FOOTBALL  SEASON TICKET

THE ULTIMATE FAN GUIDE

BY WILL GRAVES

First Edition
First Printing, 2019

Book design by Sarah Taplin
Cover design by Sarah Taplin
Photographs ©: Kevin Terrell/AP Images, cover (top); Don Wright/AP Images, cover (bottom left); Matt York/AP Images, cover (bottom right top); Peter Read Miller/AP Images, cover (bottom right bottom); LM Otero/AP Images, 4; Focus on Sport/Getty Images, 7, 12, 43, 51, 64, 68, 80; Icon Sportswire/Getty Images, 9; Anthony Behar/Sipa/AP Images, 10–11; Pro Football Hall of Fame/AP Images, 14, 20, 28; NFL Photos/AP Images, 16–17, 34, 38; AP Images, 22, 26; Vic Stein/Getty Images, 30; Herb Scharfman/Sports Imagery/Getty Images, 37; Donald Miralle/Getty Images, 45; Nate Fine/Getty Images, 46; Andy Lyons/Getty Images, 53, 87; Tony Tomsic/AP Images, 54; E.L. Bakke/Getty Images, 59; Mike Ehrmann/Getty Images, 62; Kirby Lee/Getty Images, 71; Jon Durr/Getty Images, 72; Elsa/Getty Images, 75; Allen Kee/Getty Images, 79; Mark Brettingen/Getty Images, 83; Bob Levey/Getty Images, 88; Dustin Bradford/Getty Images, 92; Scott Cunningham/Getty Images, 94–95; Red Line Editorial, 96–97, 103

Design Elements ©: Shutterstock Images

Press Box Books, an imprint of Press Room Editions

Library of Congress Control Number: 2018940605

ISBN:
978-1-63494-036-8 (paperback)
978-1-63494-041-2 (epub)
978-1-63494-046-7 (hosted ebook)

Distributed by North Star Editions, Inc.
2297 Waters Drive
Mendota Heights, MN 55120
www.northstareditions.com

Printed in the United States of America

TABLE OF CONTENTS

CHAPTER 1

A SUPER HOLIDAY

You won't find it on an official calendar, but make no mistake: the world stops for "Super Sunday."

Since the first Super Bowl was held in January 1967, Super Sunday has become more than just a game. Famous singers step forward to belt out the national anthem. The hottest entertainers line up to perform during the halftime show. Companies scramble to come up with inventive commercials that will have people talking long after the final whistle.

At the heart of it, though, is the game itself. Featuring the two best teams in the National Football League (NFL), the Super Bowl is the pinnacle of the sport. And when it's done, the winners get to crown themselves champions, grab the Vince Lombardi Trophy, and revel in a sea of confetti.

A Green Bay Packers fan cheers on his team at Super Bowl XLV in February 2011.

What's not to like?

The rise of Super Sunday is like the history of the NFL itself. In the beginning, it wasn't that big a deal. The first Super Bowl wasn't even a sellout. Heck, it wasn't even called the Super Bowl. Back then it was the AFL-NFL World Championship Game.

Boring, right? Fans seemed to think so.

Even though the most expensive tickets went for $12, there were plenty of empty seats at Los Angeles Memorial Coliseum as the Green Bay Packers crushed the Kansas City Chiefs 35–10.

Though his team lost, Chiefs owner Lamar Hunt came up with an idea to make the game sound cooler the next time. He noticed his kids kept playing with a toy called a Super Ball.

"My dad said, 'Well, we need to come up with a name, something like the Super Bowl,'" Lamar Hunt Jr. said. "Then he said, 'Actually, that's not a very good name. We can come up with something better.'"

> " My dad said, 'Well, we need to come up with a name, something like the Super Bowl.' Then he said, 'Actually, that's not a very good name. We can come up with something better.'"
>
> –Lamar Hunt Jr.

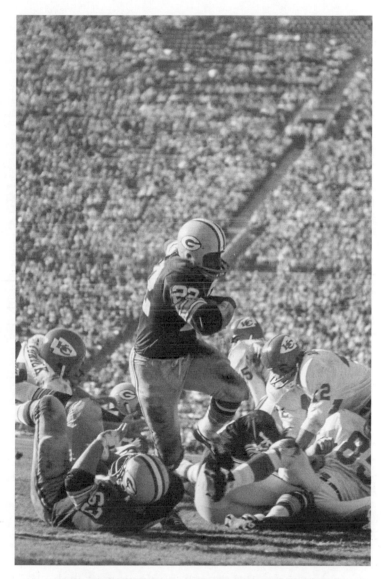

Halfback Elijah Pitts breaks through the Kansas City Chiefs defensive line during the Green Bay Packers' win in the AFL–NFL World Championship Game.

Turns out, he didn't have to.

Super Bowl sounded catchy, but it needed something more. So, Hunt also suggested adding Roman numerals for each game so fans could tell them apart. When the Baltimore Colts and Dallas Cowboys played in January 1971, it was Super Bowl V to mark the fifth Super Bowl.

As the numbers grew, so did interest in the Super Bowl. Even people who didn't regularly watch the NFL would tune in.

More than 114 million people watched when Tom Brady and the New England Patriots held on to beat the Seattle Seahawks in Super Bowl XLIX (that's 49) in February 2015. That made it the most-watched show of all time. It's a pretty safe bet that the Super Bowl will be the most-watched show of any given year.

Why all the viewers? Although the commercials and halftime show have something to do with it, mostly fans want to watch the game's best players face off on the sport's biggest stage.

The Super Bowl gives the NFL's greatest players a chance to secure their place in history. Terry Bradshaw and the "Super Steelers" brought four titles in six seasons to Pittsburgh, beginning after the 1974

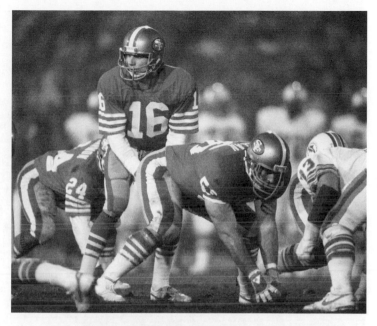

Quarterback Joe Montana and the San Francisco 49ers cemented their legacy as the team of the 1980s with four Super Bowl titles.

season. Joe Montana made winning Super Bowls look easy while quarterbacking the San Francisco 49ers to four championships of their own, beginning in the 1980s. A few decades later, in February 2017, Brady and the Patriots mounted a record-setting comeback to beat the Atlanta Falcons in Super Bowl LI. That marked Brady's fifth Super Bowl title, the most ever for a quarterback.

Pop stars Beyoncé (left) and Bruno Mars perform the halftime show at Super Bowl 50 in February 2016.

Moments outside of the game have also stood out. Singer Whitney Houston sang a pitch-perfect version of "The Star-Spangled Banner" as fans waved US flags before Super Bowl XXV. That game, in January 1991, came just as the United States began to fight Iraq

in the Gulf War. Two years later, pop icon Michael Jackson seemingly appeared all over the Rose Bowl during the Super Bowl XXVII halftime show via body doubles. Since then, the halftime performer has been a who's who of famous singers, featuring everyone from Bruce Springsteen to Lady Gaga.

11

> The Patriots' Malcolm Butler snags an interception at
> the goal line to save Super Bowl XLIX for his team.

Yet the Super Bowl doesn't just focus on the superstar players and famous entertainers. It also gives players you've never heard of a chance to claim their spot in history.

New York Giants wide receiver David Tyree had four catches during the entire 2007 regular season. In Super Bowl XLII, he used his helmet to help make a miracle catch to help New York score a shocking upset against the unbeaten Patriots. Twenty years earlier, in January 1988, little-used Washington Redskins rookie running back Timmy Smith carved up the Denver Broncos for 204 yards rushing and two touchdowns in Super Bowl XXII. And in February 2015, undrafted cornerback Malcolm Butler of the Patriots picked off Seattle's Russell Wilson at the goal line late in Super Bowl XLIX to help New England edge the Seahawks 28–24 in a thrilling finish. Three years later, backup quarterback Nick Foles led the Philadelphia Eagles to their first Super Bowl win.

The Super Bowl brings something for everyone. Whether fans or friends, Super Sunday is a time when people get together to take in the best of the best in America's most popular sport.

CHAPTER 2

LEATHER HELMETS AND IRON MEN

There was no NFL in 1892. No Super Bowl. No video games. No family dinners scheduled around Sunday afternoon kickoffs. No tailgating, either.

Football was still trying to find its footing in the 1890s, a time when the horse and buggy was still the best way to get around. A mixture of soccer and rugby, football had a hard time competing with other sports for popularity in the United States.

Baseball clubs were springing up along the East Coast. Horse racing fans flocked to the local track to place their bets. Thousands turned out for heavyweight boxing fights. Football, with its rugged

 William "Pudge" Heffelfinger became the first professional football player in 1892.

Jim Thorpe (left), a Hall of Famer best known as a halfback, prepares to make a tackle during a game in the early 1920s.

tackling and frequently changing rules, was reserved for high school and college players.

Then William "Pudge" Heffelfinger came along.

Heffelfinger was a standout player for Yale University. He joined the Allegheny (Pennsylvania) Athletic Association for a game against the Pittsburgh Athletic Club on November 12, 1892. Allegheny wanted

the 6-foot-3, 200-pound Heffelfinger on the team so badly that it offered him $500 to suit up. Heffelfinger gladly cashed in, and pro football was born.

The Pittsburgh Athletic Club played Allegheny to a 6–6 tie. The next year, Pittsburgh signed running back Grant Dibert to the first known contract, and in 1905, the Canton (Ohio) Athletic Club decided to pay everyone on the team, becoming the game's first truly professional team.

The game back then looked far different from the one we know today.

Early on, a forward pass of any kind was illegal. Field goals were worth four points, not three as they are now. Most players were required to play both offense and defense, and fans called them "iron men" because they never left the field during a game. Even quarterbacks played both ways. One of the NFL's earliest stars, Sammy Baugh, a quarterback for the Washington Redskins in the 1930s and 1940s, also punted and played safety.

The uniforms were different, too. Instead of the hard plastic helmets with face masks designed to provide maximum protection, equipment in the days of Heffelfinger and Dibert was primitive.

The first helmet was invented out of desperation. Joseph Mason Reeves was a cadet at the US Naval Academy and a member of its football team in 1893. Navy was preparing for its annual showdown with Army, but Reeves's doctor was worried about Reeve getting hit in the head too many times. The doctor told Reeve he needed to find a way to protect himself. Reeve did. He found a shoemaker who created a moleskin hat that Reeve could pull over his head.

Helmets weren't used regularly until about 1920, and because they were made of leather, players became known as "leatherheads." Just like the helmets, the pads the players wore were crude and didn't offer much protection.

Still, fans started to take notice.

Teams were formed in Ohio, Indiana, New York, and Illinois. Representatives from the group met in Canton, Ohio, in 1920 and decided to create a league. They called it the American Professional Football Association (APFA).

While college football games at the time were played in massive stadiums packed with tens of thousands of people, the APFA played in smaller venues.

The Green Bay Packers joined the league in 1921 and played their first two seasons at Hagemeister Park. At first, Hagemeister Park was just an open field. The city decided to build a fence around it so fans would have to pay to watch. A set of bleachers that could seat 1,500 fans was added. Compare that to the current home of the Packers, Lambeau Field, which can hold more than 81,000 "Cheeseheads" (a popular nickname for Green Bay fans) for a game.

Hall of Fame center George Trafton played in 1920 for the Decatur Staleys, who became today's Chicago Bears.

In the summer of 1922, the APFA came up with a catchier name: the National Football League.

The name stuck.

There were plenty of struggles in the league's early days. Teams would pop up for a few seasons, then go out of business. The Columbus (Ohio) Tigers were part of the original 14-team APFA. They went 0–9 in 1925, scoring just 28 points all season. The Tigers were 1–6 in 1926 when they folded before the season was over.

Still, there were success stories. Those early struggles in Green Bay faded quickly. As the 1920s turned into the 1930s, the Packers became a powerhouse.

The league also found stability in larger cities such as Chicago and New York. What the NFL really needed, though, were stars.

Turns out, they were on the way.

CHAPTER 3

OLD SCHOOL GREATS

George Halas didn't invent the NFL. It just seems that way. The man they called "Papa Bear" began his long relationship with the Chicago Bears in 1920, when the team played in Decatur, Illinois, and was known as the Staleys. Halas spent his first eight seasons with the team as player/coach. In many ways, he was ahead of his time.

Halas was the first coach to schedule daily practices. He was the first to make sure games were broadcast on the radio. Halas also understood the best way to get people to show up to games was to make sure there were players they wanted to see.

College football ruled in the 1920s, and Harold

George Halas was involved with the Chicago Bears from 1920 until his death in 1983.

"Red" Grange, a running back at Illinois, was one of its biggest stars. He was nicknamed the "Galloping Ghost" because of the way he could run away from opponents. During a game against Michigan in 1924, Grange scored six touchdowns. Four of those came from 40 yards or farther.

Halas wanted Grange to bring his talent and his star power to the NFL. The Bears, who moved to Chicago in 1921 and took on that name in 1922, wasted little time. Grange signed with the Bears in 1925, one day after his final college game. Four days after that, Grange played his first NFL game. A crowd of 36,000 fans showed up at Wrigley Field to watch Grange play running back and defensive back for the Bears that day. Soon after, 70,000 turned up for a game in New York to see Grange go to work against the Giants. He sealed a 19–7 Chicago win with a 35-yard interception return for a touchdown in the fourth quarter.

The NFL had its first real star. Grange spent most of his career with the Bears before retiring after the 1934 season. Although he was never quite the same after suffering a knee injury in 1927, he gave the NFL the very thing Halas said it needed: somebody to watch.

"He was the maker of professional football because of what he added to it," Halas said.

Soon, other high-profile college players began making their way to the NFL.

Bronko Nagurski was such a complete player that his college coach at Minnesota thought the burly 6-foot-2, 226-pounder could have excelled at whatever position he wanted. Halas chose to put Nagurski at fullback and along the defensive line.

Nagurski's straight-ahead running style made him the perfect symbol for a league trying to make a name for itself. He didn't run away from defenders. He wanted to run through them. The more players who tried to hit him, the better.

> " There was something strange about tackling Nagurski. When you hit him at the ankles, it is almost like getting an electric shock. If you hit him above the ankles, you are likely to get killed."
>
> –Red Grange

"There was something strange about tackling Nagurski," said Grange, who played alongside Nagurski for the Bears during the 1930s. "When you hit him at the ankles, it is almost like getting an electric shock.

Bears superstars Red Grange (left) and Bronko Nagurski pose for a picture in the 1930s.

If you hit him above the ankles, you are likely to get killed."

Nagurski wasn't just a devastating runner and a crushing blocker. He could throw the ball, too. And one famous pass changed the course of the sport's future.

NFL rules in the early 1930s stated a player had to be at least five yards behind the line of scrimmage to throw a pass. Nagurski ignored the rules in the 1932 NFL title game. Bad weather forced the Bears to play Portsmouth (Ohio) on a makeshift indoor field that stretched only 80 yards instead of the usual 100.

Scoring was tough. So, with the ball at the Portsmouth 1-yard line in the fourth quarter, Nagurski came up with an idea. He took the snap, faked a run and jumped in the air to throw a pass to a wide-open Grange.

Portsmouth complained that Nagurski wasn't far enough behind the line of scrimmage. It didn't matter; the score counted, and the NFL was changed forever.

Before the next season, the league tweaked the rules to allow players to throw the ball from anywhere behind the line of scrimmage. It set the floodgates open for quarterbacks to start chucking the ball all over the field and created a new kind of weapon: the wide receiver.

> The Packers' Don Hutson catches a pass against the Washington Redskins in 1941.

Don Hutson was one of the first players to define the position. Hutson had been a standout during his college days at Alabama and signed with the Green Bay Packers before the 1935 season. It didn't take him long to turn heads. He scored a touchdown the first time he ever caught a pass, hauling in an 83-yard bomb against Chicago. The sight of Hutson sprinting to the end zone became a fixture at Green Bay games over the next decade. He scored 99 touchdowns during his career and invented many of the pass patterns players at all levels use today. Hutson's ability to fake out a defender made it nearly impossible to cover him.

"I just concede him two touchdowns a game, and I hope we can score more," Halas said.

Hutson, like all wide receivers, still needed someone to throw the ball. That's where quarterbacks came in. When the NFL began, quarterbacks were treated mostly like just another running back. The ability to throw the ball downfield helped turn the quarterback into one of the most important positions in all of sports.

"Slinging" Sammy Baugh was the first NFL quarterback to truly master the art of passing. During his 16 seasons with the Washington Redskins, Baugh led the league in passing yards six times. He was also an excellent punter and defensive back. The Redskins won two titles during Baugh's career, including a 28–21 upset of the Bears in the 1937 championship game. Despite playing in frigid conditions, Baugh threw for a whopping 335 yards and three touchdowns.

"Baugh was a one-man team," a Bears coach told reporters after the game. "He licked us all by himself."

CHAPTER 4

RIVALRIES, THEN MERGERS

By the 1940s, the NFL was a thriving business. The league found stability in places like Chicago, New York, and Washington, D.C. Stadiums were full on Sundays. Fans were happy. Owners were making money, and interest in professional football was growing. Naturally, other cities wanted to get in on the action.

Some tried to join the NFL. Others joined together to form their own leagues, hoping the NFL would take notice. The first real rival to the NFL arrived in the late 1940s. Arch Ward, a newspaper editor in Chicago, encouraged a group of businessmen to challenge the NFL. The All-American Football Conference (AAFC)

Otto Graham and the Cleveland Browns dominated the AAFC, winning four championships in a row from 1946 to 1949.

came to life in 1946 and featured teams in places the NFL didn't play, such as Miami and San Francisco.

The AAFC lasted four years but was unable to consistently sign the top players in the country. The AAFC went out of business after the 1949 season. It wasn't a total loss, though. The Baltimore Colts, Cleveland Browns, and San Francisco 49ers moved over to the NFL in 1950.

The Browns had won the AAFC title during each of the league's four seasons. Still, most NFL fans thought the AAFC teams were inferior.

One game changed that. The Browns met the two-time defending NFL champion Philadelphia Eagles in the 1950 season opener. Most fans thought it would be a mismatch. They were right. But it was the Eagles who couldn't keep up with the Browns.

Browns quarterback Otto Graham passed for 346 yards and three touchdowns in a 35–10 victory. Cleveland went on to become NFL champions, beating the Los Angeles Rams 30–28 in the 1950 title game. It was sweet revenge for Cleveland. The Rams had originally played in Cleveland before heading west to California after the 1945 season.

Although the Browns won the battle, the NFL won the war, because it no longer had to compete with the

AAFC. However, an even bigger fight loomed in the 1960s—one that changed the landscape of professional football for good.

Lamar Hunt loved football. He loved it so much he wanted to bring a pro team to Dallas. One problem: The NFL kept saying no.

So Hunt did more than get mad. He got even.

The 26-year-old Hunt brought together other businessmen to form a league of their own. They called it the American Football League (AFL).

The AFL started in 1960 with eight teams, including Hunt's Dallas Texans. The AFL wanted to create a product that was more exciting than the NFL. There was more passing in the AFL. The AFL adopted a two-point conversion like the one used in college and signed a television deal with ABC so the league's games could compete head-to-head on Sundays against the NFL games on CBS.

The biggest rivalry in the history of pro football was born.

Though the owners in the two leagues said they wouldn't try to lure players from one league to the other, the rules didn't apply to college players.

Soon, the NFL and AFL were locked in a bidding war for the best college prospects.

Both leagues wanted Joe Namath in the 1964 draft, but the Alabama quarterback picked the AFL's New York Jets.

The two leagues held their own player drafts, and often the same players would be selected by both an AFL team and an NFL team, giving the player the freedom to sign with the club that offered him the most money.

Things quickly got out of hand.

On November 28, 1964, the AFL and NFL held their drafts on the same day. The AFL's New York Jets took Alabama quarterback Joe Namath with the first overall pick. The St. Louis Cardinals grabbed Namath with the 12th overall pick in the NFL Draft.

Namath asked the Cardinals for a contract that would pay him $200,000 a year. The quarterback with the movie-star good looks and massive arm asked for a new car, too.

The Jets had no problem giving "Broadway Joe" whatever he wanted, and he signed a three-year, $427,000 deal with New York on January 2, 1965. The signing shook the NFL owners, who wanted to keep player contracts under control.

"Contracts like the one Namath got can be the ruination of the game," a fuming Cleveland Browns owner Art Modell said.

In a way, however, Namath's contract might have

saved the game rather than ruining it. Something had to change. Teams were spending so much money to land the best players that they risked going out of business.

Realizing it might not be able to run the AFL out of business, the NFL decided a merger of the two leagues would make pro football stronger than ever.

> 66 Contracts like the one Namath got can be the ruination of the game."
> —Cleveland Browns owner Art Modell

The rivals reached an agreement in the summer of 1966, announcing they would form into a new-look NFL in 1970. Every AFL team would move to the NFL and play in the newly formed American Football Conference (AFC). That group included Hunt's franchise, which had moved from Dallas to Kansas City in 1963 and renamed itself the Chiefs. Three existing NFL teams—the Pittsburgh Steelers, Baltimore Colts, and Cleveland Browns—also moved to the AFC.

Part of the deal included an annual championship game, beginning in the 1966 season. At first, this game featured the AFL and NFL winners. After the merger

> **Len Dawson (16) of the Kansas City Chiefs hands off to Mike Garrett against the Buffalo Bills during the AFL Championship Game on January 1, 1967.**

was completed in 1970, the AFC winner took on the National Football Conference (NFC) winner.

You now know this game as the Super Bowl.

37

CHAPTER 5

GROWING THE GAME

By the 1950s, pro football was closing in on Major League Baseball as the top sport in the United States.

Televisions were popping up in living rooms across the country, replacing radio as the preferred way to take in a game. NFL owners soon realized the best way to attract new fans was by making sure their games were shown on television.

The 1951 NFL Championship Game between Cleveland and Los Angeles became the first to be aired live across the country. Folks tuned in to see the Rams edge the Browns 24–17.

Progress came slowly. What the league really needed was one moment to capture the public's

 Los Angeles Rams quarterback Bob Waterfield jumps over Cleveland Browns defenders during the 1951 NFL Championship Game.

imagination. That moment arrived on December 28, 1958, when the Baltimore Colts traveled to New York to face the Giants in the title game.

Young quarterback Johnny Unitas led the Colts. The Pittsburgh Steelers had drafted him in 1955, but they cut him. He ended up playing in a semi-pro league around Pittsburgh for $6 a game before Baltimore coach Weeb Ewbank decided to take a chance on the tall kid with the cannon for an arm.

By 1958, "Johnny U" was the top quarterback in the NFL, and the Colts were ready to challenge the Giants for league supremacy. New York had some of the league's biggest stars, including running back Frank Gifford and linebacker Sam Huff.

While millions watched on TV, the Giants took a 17–14 lead into the final minutes. Then Unitas went to work. He led Baltimore on a long drive, connecting with wide receiver Raymond Berry three times for 62 yards as the clock ticked toward zero. With 10 seconds remaining, Colts kicker Steve Myhra booted a 20-yard field goal to tie the score.

Then things got wild.

Up until that time, every game in pro football history was over at the end of the fourth quarter, no matter the score. If the score was tied, the game was ruled a tie.

That can't happen during the playoffs. For the first time ever, an NFL game was going to overtime.

The Giants got the ball first and punted. New York never got it back.

Unitas guided Baltimore down the field to the New York 1-yard line. On third down, he handed the ball off to Alan Ameche, and the fullback tumbled forward into the end zone for the winning score.

"If they play pro football for 100 years, they never can top Baltimore's first championship snatched dramatically in a sudden-death playoff," the Associated Press wrote after the game. "It seems pro football has come of age."

The nation had a new favorite sport. Fans couldn't get enough football. The rise of television helped the AFL succeed where other rival leagues had failed.

When the AFL and NFL merged in 1970, the NFL searched for new ways to bring the game to fans. They found their answer on Monday nights.

For the first 50 years of the league, games were played almost exclusively on Sundays. Then the NFL approached television networks about doing a special game during the week. Both NBC and CBS said no.

ABC said yes, and *Monday Night Football* was born.

Every week, millions would tune in to watch the Monday night game. For many, it was the biggest game of the week. Advances in technology gave fans an up-close view of the game. Instant replay allowed viewers to get a close look at what just happened in slow motion. Decades later, *Monday Night Football* remains a fixture. The league has also added weekly games on Thursday and Sunday nights for fans who can't get enough of the game.

In 1962, the league established NFL Films. Film crews worked the sideline at every game. Directors set their highlights to music and used a narrator to weave stories of teams and seasons into mini-movies that gave viewers a behind-the-scenes look at the game.

The crews didn't lack for good stories to tell.

During the 1960s, the Green Bay Packers and hard-driving coach Vince Lombardi became football's gold standard. Led by quarterback Bart Starr and a defense that featured gritty linebacker Ray Nitschke, the Packers won three NFL titles and drilled Kansas City and Oakland in the first two Super Bowls.

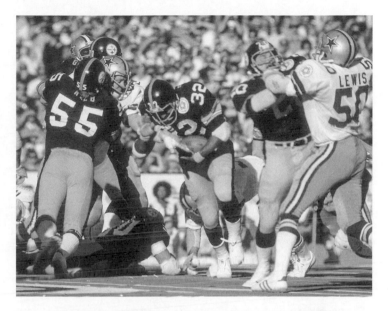

Franco Harris (32) and the Steelers ran to another
championship at Super Bowl X in January 1976.

The 1970s saw the rise of the Pittsburgh Steelers.
Coach Chuck Noll built a "Steel Curtain" defense
around lineman "Mean" Joe Green. Quarterback Terry
Bradshaw, running back Franco Harris, and wide
receivers John Stallworth and Lynn Swann took care
of the offense. With their fans waving their yellow
Terrible Towels at Three Rivers Stadium, the Steelers
won four Super Bowls in six years during the 1970s.

The 1980s belonged to coach Bill Walsh, quarterback
Joe Montana, and the San Francisco 49ers. With "Joe

Cool" throwing to wide receivers Dwight Clark and Jerry Rice, the 49ers won four Super Bowls between the 1981 and 1989 seasons.

The Dallas Cowboys were contenders nearly every year throughout the 1970s and early 1980s thanks to coach Tom Landry, who roamed the sideline in his trademark fedora hat. The Cowboys posted a winning record 20 straight seasons between 1966 and 1985. Their success earned them the nickname "America's Team." Not everyone in America, though, rooted for the guys in the silver helmets with the blue star on the side.

After a downturn in the late 1980s, the Cowboys, led by "The Triplets," were back in the 1990s. No, they weren't babies. The Triplets were quarterback Troy Aikman, running back Emmitt Smith, and wide receiver Michael Irvin. They guided the Cowboys to three Super Bowls in four years.

The 2000s saw the rise of the New England Patriots and quarterback Tom Brady. Brady and gruff coach Bill Belichick pulled off an upset in Super Bowl XXXVI after the 2001 season. Over the course of the next 16 years, they won four more Super Bowls and played in three others.

No quarterback has won more Super Bowls than the New England Patriots' Tom Brady.

While New England fans celebrated their team's success, fans of other teams came together to root against them. When the Patriots played Atlanta in Super Bowl LI in February 2017, only a quarter of the people in the United States were pulling for the Pats.

Either way, people watched. The game drew 111.3 million viewers on TV. Not everyone went home happy. The Patriots rallied from a 25-point deficit to win in overtime.

Nearly 60 years after Johnny U and the Colts brought the game to the masses, interest in the NFL was still growing.

CHAPTER 6

MAGNIFICENT MAESTROS

There are 22 players on the field during every foot ball play. All have different jobs. Wide receivers run pass routes. Running backs carry the ball. Offensive linemen block. The 11 players on defense do what they can to stop whoever has the ball.

Every job is important. For teams to win, every player needs to do his job the right way.

One job, however, stands above the rest: quarterback.

One of the most glamorous roles in sports didn't start out that way. Back in football's early days, quarterbacks were basically running backs. They would

Washington Redskins quarterback "Slingin'" Sammy Baugh revolutionized the position with his passing.

get the snap from the center and take off with the ball, or they'd hand it to a teammate and turn into a blocker.

Things changed in the early 1930s. The league relaxed the passing rules. Coaches realized throwing the ball was a good way to get downfield quickly. It didn't take long for coaches to convince their quarterbacks that putting the ball in the air was a good idea.

Before Sammy Baugh arrived in the NFL with the Washington Redskins in 1937, no quarterback had ever passed for more than 1,239 yards in a season. Baugh topped that number three times in his first seven seasons, and the Redskins kept winning.

Pretty soon, balls were flying in stadiums all over the NFL. The passing game gave quarterbacks freedom. Most called their own plays back then. Many loved nothing more than to chuck it downfield to an open teammate, though they did it in a variety of ways.

Otto Graham rose to stardom playing for the Cleveland Browns in the 1940s and 1950s. When the Browns moved from the AAFC to the NFL in 1950, some thought the high-flying offense Graham led in the AAFC wouldn't work.

They were wrong. Graham and Cleveland appeared

in the NFL title game every year between 1950 and 1955, winning it three times.

"The test of a quarterback is where his team finishes," said Paul Brown, who coached Graham during his pro career. "By that standard, Otto Graham was the best of all time."

The standards, though, were continually being raised.

Johnny Unitas became the godfather of the no-huddle "two-minute drill." His heroics against the New York Giants in the 1958 title game brought the thrill of NFL football to the masses. Unitas was a gunslinger of sorts. Wearing black high-top cleats, he loved to stand in the pocket and rifle the ball into tight spots. He played with swagger, but some of his peers were a bit more buttoned down.

Vince Lombardi didn't ask Bart Starr to go out and win games. The Packers were so successful in the 1960s that the game was usually well in hand by the time the two-minute warning came around. Starr didn't put up eye-popping numbers. He focused on

> " The test of a quarterback is where his team finishes. By that standard, Otto Graham was the best of all time."
> —Browns coach Paul Brown

making sure the team followed Lombardi's game plan. Starr considered himself a "coach on the field." He thought leadership was just as important as a great arm. Starr would do whatever it took to win. Maybe that's why his most famous play was a 1-yard run.

The Packers were playing the Dallas Cowboys in the 1967 NFL title game, known as the "Ice Bowl" because the temperature at kickoff was minus 13 degrees. The Packers trailed 17–14 late but had the ball at the Dallas 1. Time was running out. Green Bay could attempt a field goal to tie the score or go for the win.

During a timeout, Starr told Lombardi a regular running play wouldn't work because the ground was slippery. He suggested a quarterback sneak. Lombardi told Starr to run the play and score so the game would end and they could get out of the cold. Starr took the snap and stretched forward into the end zone. The Packers were on their way to a second Super Bowl victory, and Starr's legacy was set.

Starr might have been one of the last old-school quarterbacks. By the late 1960s, new faces were on the scene, as was a new way of playing the position. Joe Namath and the New York Jets were a perfect match. "Broadway Joe" looked like a movie star, wore fancy

 Fran Tarkenton retired in 1978 with career passing
records for completions, yards, and touchdowns.

clothes, and never had a problem posing in front of
a camera.

Oh, and he could throw the ball. Namath became
the first quarterback to top 4,000 yards passing in a
season when he threw for 4,007 yards in 1967. That
season ended with Namath leading New York to one
of the biggest upsets in history when the Jets beat the
Baltimore Colts 16–7 in Super Bowl III.

Quarterbacks don't just make plays with their
arms, but also with their legs. Fran Tarkenton and
Roger Staubach proved it while playing in the 1960s
and 1970s. Tarkenton was known for his scrambling
ability. He would run all over the field to escape

hard-charging defensive linemen while playing for the Minnesota Vikings and New York Giants. Staubach was known as "Roger the Dodger" because of his ability to outrun defenders.

Still, nearly every championship team felt it needed to rely on a solid running game to win. The Cowboys of the 1970s had backs like Calvin Hill and Tony Dorsett. Meanwhile, Terry Bradshaw had Franco Harris and Rocky Bleier to hand the ball to during the "Super Steelers" era of the 1970s.

That changed in the 1980s, thanks to San Francisco 49ers coach Bill Walsh and a skinny quarterback from Notre Dame named Joe Montana.

Walsh came up with an offensive scheme called the West Coast Offense. Rather than throw the ball deep all the time, Walsh wanted Montana to control the game with short passes that the San Francisco receivers could turn into long gains.

Along with talented wideout Jerry Rice, Montana and the 49ers didn't need a burly running back. San Francisco won with precision passing.

In the 1990s, Green Bay's Brett Favre was a throwback. He would often run around like a kid in a flag football game looking to make a play. He made

Peyton Manning threw 539 touchdown passes over 266 games, averaging more than two per game.

plenty of them en route to setting NFL records for touchdown passes and yards passing.

The records didn't last long. Peyton Manning broke both of them while playing for Indianapolis and Denver before retiring after the Broncos won Super Bowl 50 in January 2016. With Tom Brady still going strong at age 40 in 2017, Manning's records may be in jeopardy.

For proof of how the game has evolved since Sammy Baugh broke into the NFL, look at the records. When Baugh retired in 1952, his career passing total of 21,886 yards was a record. Compare that to Manning's mark of 71,940 yards. That's more than 28 miles longer than Baugh's mark!

CHAPTER 7

GAME-CHANGING GAMES

The 1958 NFL title game was an overtime classic that helped usher the league into a new era of popularity. That popularity has only grown. A few unforgettable games paved the way.

SUPER BOWL III, JANUARY 12, 1969

Going into year three, people weren't quite sure what to think about the Super Bowl. The established NFL champ had walloped the AFL champ in the first two games. There was little reason to think anything would be different in Super Bowl III.

A bold prediction from Joe Namath changed everything. The Baltimore Colts were favored to beat

 Joe Namath and the New York Jets stunned fans with their upset win in Super Bowl III.

the New York Jets by 18 points. Namath didn't care. He told reporters a few days before the game in Miami that his Jets would win. In fact, he guaranteed it.

Suddenly the game took on a new level of intrigue. People all across the country tuned in to see if "Broadway Joe" and the upstart Jets could pull it off.

Namath's numbers weren't flashy. But a strong running game and stout defense kept the Colts off balance all game, and the Jets won 16–7. The AFL finally showed it could hang with the NFL. Namath celebrated by running off the field at the Orange Bowl with his right index finger in the air.

The Jets were indeed number one. Just like Namath said they would be.

THE IMMACULATE RECEPTION, DECEMBER 23, 1972

The Pittsburgh Steelers joined the NFL in 1933. In their first 39 seasons, they did not win a playoff game. Then Franco Harris found himself in the right place at the right time in an ending that changed the Steelers' fortunes for good.

Pittsburgh trailed the Oakland Raiders 7–6 late in the fourth quarter of a divisional playoff game.

Terry Bradshaw heaved a long pass to running back John "Frenchy" Fuqua. Oakland cornerback Jack Tatum hit Fuqua just as the pass arrived. The ball deflected high in the air. Harris raced in, snagged the ball just before it hit the ground, and raced down the sideline for the game-winning 60-yard touchdown as the Three Rivers Stadium crowd erupted.

> **"** I've played football since the second grade and nothing like that ever happened. It'll never happen again."
> —Steelers quarterback Terry Bradshaw

"I've played football since the second grade and nothing like that ever happened," Bradshaw said. "It'll never happen again."

THE CATCH, JANUARY 10, 1982

The San Francisco 49ers were in trouble. They needed a touchdown against the Dallas Cowboys late in the fourth quarter of the NFC Championship Game. The winner would go to the Super Bowl.

San Francisco faced third down at the Dallas 6. Joe Montana took the snap and scrambled to his right with two Dallas players in hot pursuit. Montana faked a pass to make the defenders jump. Then he let loose with a pass that sailed toward the back corner of the end zone.

It looked as if the ball would go into the first row of the stands.

Wrong.

San Francisco wide receiver Dwight Clark reached high in the air and grabbed it. When he landed, the 49ers were on their way to the first of their four Super Bowls over the next decade. It all started with the biggest play of Clark's career.

"It was a double-catch," Clark said. "I knocked it down. My hands were flat. It was a perfect throw and just how [49ers head coach] Bill [Walsh] told him how to do it."

And a perfect ending for the 49ers.

THE DRIVE, JANUARY 11, 1987

The Denver Broncos had a long way to go and a short time to get there. The Broncos were down by a touchdown and had the ball at their own 2 with just over five minutes to go in the AFC Championship Game against Cleveland.

Then John Elway took over.

The quarterback slowly, steadily took the Broncos down the field. He converted a third-and-18 pass to keep the drive alive and tied the score with a bullet 5-yard pass to Vance Johnson with 37 seconds left. The

There was no stopping John Elway and the Broncos during "The Drive" against the Cleveland Browns.

Broncos won on an overtime field goal, and Elway's NFL legend was born.

> 66 I've never seen John cooler than he was when he came into the huddle at the 2. In fact, I've never seen anybody cooler in such a pressure situation."
>
> —Broncos wide receiver Steve Watson

"I've never seen John cooler than he was when he came into the huddle at the 2," Broncos wide receiver Steve Watson said. "In fact, I've never seen anybody cooler in such a pressure situation."

Maybe because when it came to Elway, cool was the rule.

THE COMEBACK, JANUARY 3, 1993

The Buffalo Bills appeared to be done. No team comes back when it's trailing 35–3 in the second half, especially with its starting quarterback out. Then again, Frank Reich wasn't just any backup quarterback. While playing in college at Maryland, he led the Terrapins back from 31 points down to beat mighty Miami. It was the greatest comeback in college football history at the time.

Reich one-upped himself in the first round of the 1993 playoffs. The two-time defending AFC champions were on the ropes when the Houston Oilers returned a Reich interception for a touchdown to go up by 32 points.

Then Reich went to work. He threw four touchdown passes in the second half to spark an impossible rally. Buffalo won on a field goal in overtime after one of the unlikeliest comebacks ever.

THE HELMET CATCH, FEBRUARY 3, 2008

The New England Patriots were on the verge of making history. They had gone through the regular season unbeaten. Now they were minutes from becoming the first NFL team ever to go 19–0 and just the second to ever have an undefeated season.

Little-known New York Giants wide receiver David Tyree and his helmet helped put a stop to New England's run at perfection.

The Giants were down 14–10 late in the fourth quarter. Quarterback Eli Manning broke loose from the New England pass rush and launched the ball toward Tyree in the middle of the field.

With New England defensive back Rodney Harrison all over him, Tyree pinned the ball to his helmet with his hand and held on as he tumbled to the ground for a 32-yard gain.

Tom Brady celebrates winning his fifth championship with the New England Patriots at Super Bowl LI in February 2017.

New York scored the go-ahead touchdown four plays later. The Giants won thanks to Tyree's improbable heroics.

THE COMEBACK, PART 2, FEBRUARY 5, 2017

Nothing went right for the New England Patriots in the first 2 ½ quarters of Super Bowl LI. The odds seemed stacked against them as they fell behind 28–3 to the Atlanta Falcons.

A big dose of Tom Brady magic (and a little bit of luck) started the biggest rally in Super Bowl history. The Patriots scored 25 points over the final 17 minutes of regulation to force overtime. One of the key plays came on a juggling catch in the middle of the field by wide receiver Julian Edelman. The ball was tipped by a Falcons defender, but Edelman fought off three Atlanta players to grab it just before it hit the ground.

The Patriots tied the score four plays later and won in overtime to add another point to the argument that Brady is the greatest quarterback of all time.

CHAPTER 8

DYNASTIES

Every NFL season ends with one team celebrating under an avalanche of confetti with the Vince Lombardi Trophy in hand as league champions.

All champions, though, are not created equal.

Some teams find a way to stick around for a while, winning multiple championships and establishing themselves as dynasties.

The NFL's first dynasty was one of its founding teams. George Halas joined the Decatur Staleys during their first season in 1920. The team moved to Chicago in 1921 and became the Bears in 1922. Halas was there all the while. In fact, Halas stuck with the team as a player, coach, and then owner until his death in 1983.

As a coach, Halas demanded his players be tough. His "Monsters of the Midway" played a physical style

 Quarterback Bart Starr and the Green Bay Packers dominated the NFL in the 1960s.

that few teams could match. And in 1939, Halas found the right quarterback to go with it in Sid Luckman. The Bears reached the NFL title game each year between 1940 and 1943, winning twice.

These Bears are best remembered for their performance in the 1940 NFL title game when they beat Washington 73–0. It's still the biggest blowout in NFL history.

Another coach helped turn the Bears' northern rivals into the team to beat during the 1960s. The Green Bay Packers had been one of the NFL's first powerhouses, winning five titles between 1929 and 1939. By the late 1950s, though, the team was a mess.

> **" I have never been on a losing team, gentlemen, and I do not intend to start now!"**
> —Packers coach Vince Lombardi

The Packers needed a new voice. They found one in coach Vince Lombardi. When Lombardi introduced himself to his players after he was hired in 1959, he made it clear he meant business.

"I have never been on a losing team, gentlemen, and I do not intend to start now!" Lombardi said.

He wasn't kidding.

The Packers improved from 1–10–1 the year before Lombardi arrived to 7–5 in his first season. Between 1961 and 1967, Green Bay won five NFL titles, including two Super Bowls, and never finished with a losing record. Ten Packers from that era reached the Pro Football Hall of Fame, including quarterback Bart Starr.

The Super Bowl brought newfound attention to the NFL in the late 1960s, and into the next decade, four teams attempted to take over.

The Minnesota Vikings came close. Led by the "Purple People Eaters" defense, the Vikings struck fear into opposing offenses—at least until the big game. Minnesota lost all four Super Bowls it played in during the 1970s.

One of those losses came to the Miami Dolphins in January 1974. That game also marked the end of one of the most dominant stretches in NFL history. The Dolphins had reached three consecutive Super Bowls and won two of them.

Even today, no team can match the 1972 Dolphins. With the "No Name" defense shutting down opponents and a three-headed rushing attack with Larry Csonka, Jim Kiick, and Mercury Morris running over defenders, Miami was unstoppable.

> **Running back Mercury Morris and the 1972 Miami Dolphins remain the only team to go undefeated through an entire season.**

The Dolphins won every game they played that season, including the Super Bowl, to finish 17–0. It's a feat unmatched by any NFL champion since.

Miami's only blemish during that three-year stretch was a Super Bowl loss to the Dallas Cowboys in January 1972. Led by quarterback Roger Staubach, the Cowboys won two Super Bowls and appeared in three others while becoming "America's Team" during the 1970s.

But no team was as good for as long during the decade as the Pittsburgh Steelers.

The Steelers didn't win the Super Bowl after Franco Harris' "Immaculate Reception" in the 1972 playoffs. Pittsburgh's run ended the next week with a loss to Miami in the AFC Championship Game.

Still, it set the stage for one of the most dominant stretches ever. Over the next six years, coach Chuck Noll led the Steelers to four Super Bowl titles. Pittsburgh, which had known only misery during its first 40 years in the NFL, became known as the "City of Champions."

The Steelers were built on the broad shoulders of the "Steel Curtain" defense. Defensive end "Mean" Joe Greene, linebackers Jack Lambert and Jack Ham, and defensive backs Mel Blount and Donnie Shell stuffed opponents. By the late 1970s, quarterback Terry Bradshaw and receivers Lynn Swann and John Stallworth had gotten in on the act, too.

If Pittsburgh did it on defense, the San Francisco 49ers were all about the offense during the 1980s.

The 49ers were coming off a 2–14 season when they hired Bill Walsh in 1979. Walsh was considered one of the great offensive coaches of his time. He had ideas, but he needed a quarterback. He found one in Joe Montana.

The skinny, blond-haired Montana didn't have the strongest arm, but he made up for it with amazing accuracy and smarts. Using Walsh's West Coast Offense, the 49ers quickly became the NFL's gold standard during the 1980s, winning the Super Bowl each of the four times they made the trip between the 1981 and 1989 seasons.

The Cowboys were back in the 1990s.

Led by quarterback Troy Aikman, running back Emmitt Smith, and wide receiver Michael Irvin—"the Triplets"—Dallas won three Super Bowls in four years, beginning with Super Bowl XXVII in January 1993. "America's Team" had returned to the top.

Before long, though, the Patriots had taken over the NFL.

Coach Bill Belichick's rebuilding project in New England looked as if it was in trouble early in the 2001 season. Quarterback Drew Bledsoe left the second game, an eventual loss to the New York Jets, because of an injury.

Belichick had no choice but to turn to second-year quarterback Tom Brady, whom the Patriots took with the 199th selection in the 2000 draft. Brady was considered too thin and too slow to excel in the NFL.

The experts have never been more wrong.

Brady didn't just survive that first season; he thrived. The season ended with Brady leading the Patriots to a stunning upset of the St. Louis Rams in Super Bowl XXXVI. The greatest dynasty in NFL history was born.

No coach and quarterback combination has been as
successful as the Patriots' Bill Belichick and Tom Brady.

Behind Brady's consistent passing efforts and
Belichick's creative defensive schemes, New England
won back-to-back Super Bowls after the 2003 and
2004 seasons. Their only loss in the 2007 season came
against the New York Giants in the Super Bowl. But
after another Super Bowl loss to the Giants four years
later, the Pats' run appeared to be sputtering.

Think again.

A last-second interception secured Super Bowl
victory number four over the Seattle Seahawks after
the 2014 season. Then Brady led his record-setting
comeback against the Atlanta Falcons two years later.

The NFL has seen its share of special teams over
the years. But none has quite matched up with Brady,
Belichick, and the Patriots.

CHAPTER 9

FULL CIRCLE

There is no such thing as a surefire way to the NFL. The league features players from nearly every state and several countries.

Every fall, about a million teenagers play high school football in the United States. Only about 70,000 will go on to play some level of college football. Finding a spot on a college team is easy compared to making it to the NFL. There are only about 2,000 jobs in the league, including practice squads. That means just 0.2 percent of all high school players in the country reach the pros.

Getting there takes talent, hard work, and sometimes a bit of luck. Sticking around is even harder in a league in which the average career lasts just over three seasons.

 The Philadelphia Eagles selected quarterback Carson Wentz (left) second overall in 2016.

NFL teams hire scouts to scour the country for top college players. Some players also participate in scouting combines or pro days, where they're put through a series of drills, such as the 40-yard dash and the vertical jump.

All of this work culminates in the NFL Draft, which the league holds each spring so its teams can fairly divide up the players coming in from college. The team with the worst record gets to pick first in each round, barring any trades. The draft order goes backward from there, with the Super Bowl champ picking last. That means the players considered the best prospects usually go to the worst teams.

Once the draft's seven rounds are over, undrafted players can try to sign with a team. Each NFL team starts training camp in July with 90 players on the roster. Over the course of camp, the roster is trimmed to 53 players who make the team.

The makeup of those rosters might surprise you. Often the first-round draft picks turn into good players. But some high-profile players never pan out. Other players ignored in the draft go on to become stars. Still others play a handful of seasons before retiring with little fanfare.

Despite high expectations, Ryan Leaf was unable to find success as an NFL quarterback.

Ryan Leaf entered the NFL Draft in 1998 as a big-armed quarterback from Washington State. The Indianapolis Colts had the first pick that year, and there was lengthy debate whether they would pick Leaf or Peyton Manning.

When the Colts drafted Manning, the San Diego Chargers traded with Arizona so they could scoop up Leaf with the second pick. The rivalry many expected to develop between Manning and Leaf never came to pass.

While Manning went on to become the NFL's all-time leader in passing yards and a five-time Most Valuable Player (MVP) Award winner, Leaf's career lasted just three years. The Chargers signed him to a $31 million contract but released him in 2000. After a forgettable four games with the Dallas Cowboys in 2001, Leaf was out of the NFL for good.

Four of the top five picks in the 1989 draft—Troy Aikman, Barry Sanders, Derrick Thomas, and Deion Sanders—made it to the Hall of Fame. Offensive lineman Tony Mandarich, the No. 2 pick, fell short. He spent a decade in the NFL but never turned into the star NFL scouts thought he would be coming out of college.

High draft picks usually have a better chance of succeeding in the NFL than low draft picks. But sometimes the formula turns on its head.

Tom Brady wasn't much to look at going into the 2000 NFL Draft. The Michigan quarterback was tall, skinny, and slow. He needed 5.28 seconds to complete the 40-yard dash and jumped just 24 inches. The scouts said he didn't have the arm strength to be a great quarterback.

The Patriots took a flyer on Brady in the sixth round anyway. The result? Five Super Bowl titles and counting entering the 2018 season, and a reputation as one of the biggest winners in NFL history.

Antonio Brown joined a crowded wide receiver field when the Pittsburgh Steelers took him in the sixth round of the 2010 draft. The Steelers already had three good wide receivers and a pass-catching tight end.

That didn't stop Brown from becoming one of the most productive players of his generation and the highest-paid wide receiver in the NFL. In 2017, he became the first player ever to have five straight seasons with at least 100 receptions while catching passes from Ben Roethlisberger.

Maybe the greatest underdog story was that of quarterback Kurt Warner. When Warner graduated from Northern Iowa, no NFL team wanted him. He spent part of 1994 stacking groceries in Cedar Falls, Iowa, but he never gave up on his dream.

Warner landed a job with an Arena Football League team in 1995. That led to a job in NFL Europe, where he did well enough to compete for the backup quarterback spot with the St. Louis Rams in 1998. When starter Trent Green went down with a knee injury in the 1999 preseason, Warner took over.

With his quick release, the former grocery store employee orchestrated the "Greatest Show on Turf." He twice led the high-flying Rams to the Super Bowl, winning it all in January 2000, and took the Arizona Cardinals to their only Super Bowl appearance in the 2008 season before making it to the Hall of Fame in 2017.

It all just goes to show, there is no one way to find success in the NFL.

Despite not being drafted, Kurt Warner played in three
Super Bowls and won one during a Hall of Fame career.

CHAPTER 10

NEW SCHOOL GREATS

NFL players these days are bigger, faster, and stronger than the men who pioneered the league in the early 1900s. And although the feats of greats such as Red Grange can usually be found only on grainy film, the feats of today's stars make it to high-definition TV screens and smartphones almost instantly every Sunday during the fall. These new-school players have helped make the NFL more popular than ever.

Few players lit up stadiums quite like Deion Sanders.

Sanders didn't like to tackle, which is weird for a cornerback. But being a so-so tackler never held

Deion Sanders captured fans' attention with his flashy play and flashy style in the 1990s.

him back, in part because he didn't have to do much tackling. Sanders was so good while playing for five teams between 1989 and 2005 that opposing quarterbacks were afraid to throw the ball in his direction. When they did, the man called "Primetime" made sure to put on a show. Sanders was blazing fast, and when not intercepting passes, he could be found returning kicks or even sometimes lining up as a wide receiver.

"Neon Deion" loved nothing more than running toward the end zone with the ball in his hands. He would often high-step his way down the sideline before breaking into a touchdown dance.

Sanders became one of only two players in NFL history to score a touchdown six different ways, and each one was a look-at-me masterpiece.

Detroit Lions running back Barry Sanders didn't seek out attention. But with moves like his, it was hard to look away.

Sanders had the kind of moves that left opponents grasping for air. At just 5-foot-8, Sanders used his lack of height to hide behind his blockers before sprinting into the secondary. His never-ending series of moves helped him lead the NFL in rushing four times. His

If a pass was thrown in Randy Moss' direction, the Vikings receiver usually caught it.

total of 2,053 yards in 1997 was the second-highest in NFL history at the time. Sanders was also second all-time in rushing yards when he retired at age 30.

Randy Moss might have been the NFL's perfect weapon. At 6-foot-4, the legendary wide receiver had the height of a basketball player and the speed of a track star. Figuring out the right way to cover him gave defensive coordinators nightmares.

Over the course of 14 seasons between 1998 and 2012, Moss caught 982 passes for 15,292 yards and 156 touchdowns. Though best known for his early years with the Minnesota Vikings, his 23 touchdown catches for New England during its unbeaten regular season in 2007 were the most in one season in NFL history.

Moss seemed to make a game out of trying to cover him. Usually all the quarterback had to do was lob the ball in the air in Moss' direction. It didn't matter if he was covered. Moss was so tall and could jump so high, he often came down with it. Young players watching at home took notice.

> He's Randy Moss. If you burned someone deep, you got 'Moss'd.' That's all we said growing up. That was the term."
> —Ravens wide receiver Torrey Smith

"He's Randy Moss," Baltimore Ravens wide receiver Torrey Smith said. "If you burned someone deep, you got 'Moss'd.' That's all we said growing up. That was the term."

Perhaps no position in football has evolved quite like that of the quarterback.

As quarterbacks such as Joe Montana dazzled fans with their pass-happy offenses, the NFL realized that passing is fun to watch. The league adjusted some of its rules to encourage more passing. Dan Marino, Peyton Manning, and Drew Brees were among the quarterbacks who thrived in this new era.

Nobody had seen anything quite like Marino. He joined the Miami Dolphins in 1983, and with his lightning-quick release, he began smashing NFL records. In 1984, Marino became the first quarterback to pass for more than 5,000 yards in a season. That same year he threw 48 touchdown passes, crushing the previous record of 36.

Marino retired in 1999 with his name all over the record books. But by then, Manning was already one year into his quest to rewrite them. Over 17 seasons with the Indianapolis Colts and Denver Broncos, Manning passed for a league-record 71,940 yards and 539 touchdowns.

Both Marino and Manning fit the mold of a traditional NFL quarterback: Both were tall, and neither was particularly fast. But when the ball was snapped, they knew how to control the game, stay calm in the pocket, and send a bullet to the receiver.

Brees, at 6-feet tall, didn't fit that description, at least physically. Many scouts doubted he would thrive in the NFL. But once he got an opportunity to flex his throwing arm with the San Diego Chargers and New

Orleans Saints, no one questioned his ability. Brees set an NFL record by throwing a touchdown pass in 54 straight games between 2009 and 2012 and leading the Saints to their first Super Bowl title in the process.

As football entered the 2000s, though, quarterbacking became more than just sitting in the pocket and passing. One by one, a series of dual-threat quarterbacks invaded the league.

Colin Kaepernick had been a standout baseball pitcher in high school. He was also really fast. Those skills were on display when he took over as the 49ers' starting quarterback in 2012. When he wasn't whipping passes deep down the field, Kaepernick was burning defenses with his legs. That recipe got San Francisco to the Super Bowl after the 2013 season.

On the other side of the country, Carolina Panthers quarterback Cam Newton was redefining the position in his own way. At 6-foot-5 and 260 pounds, Newton's backup plan was less about racing away from defenders and more about plowing through them.

Big, athletic players are changing the game on defense, too. J.J. Watt started his college career as a tight end at Central Michigan University. Wanting to instead play defensive end, Watt decided to

J.J. Watt's rare combination of size and athleticism has helped him thrive for the Houston Texans.

walk on to the team at Wisconsin. It was a match made in heaven. The 6-foot-6, 290-pound Watt was nearly impossible to block. He played with a reckless abandon that often ended with Watt in the backfield. After turning pro, he won the NFL Defensive Player of the Year Award three times between 2012 and 2015 and twice led the league in sacks while helping the Houston Texans become a contender in the AFC South.

CHAPTER 11

SAFETY CHECK

The NFL is filled with some of the biggest stars in sports, and every one of them plays the game with a certain risk. Pro football is a physical game. Nearly every player deals with injuries at some point in his career.

Throughout its history, the NFL has tried to adjust the rules to try to keep the game as safe as possible. A Competition Committee made up of coaches and league officials reviews video every offseason and studies injuries to see if there are certain types of plays that are more dangerous than others.

Some rule changes are big ones. In 2010, the league put in place regulations that made it illegal to hit "defenseless players" in the head. An example of a defenseless player is a receiver who is stretching to

 Hard hits are built into football, but the NFL is looking for ways to limit the most dangerous plays.

catch a pass or a quarterback who has just released the ball.

Other rules changes are smaller, such as the one passed in 2012 that requires players to wear knee and thigh pads.

The league noticed that there tended to be a lot of injuries on kickoff returns because players are running at each other at full speed. So, officials moved the kickoff line three times between 1974 and 2011, and they also moved up the starting spot after a touchback from the 20-yard line to the 25. The goal was to persuade teams to take more touchbacks.

One of the NFL's biggest challenges by the mid-2010s stemmed from the rising awareness of the dangers of concussions and other brain injuries. Concussions are traumatic brain injuries that occur from a blow to the head or violent shaking that causes the brain to move within the skull. Many football concussions are suffered during helmet-to-helmet hits. The effects can vary from headaches to nausea to a heightened sensitivity to light.

Studies have also shown that repetitive head trauma can cause Chronic Traumatic Encephalopathy (CTE). One study found CTE in the brains of 99 percent of former NFL players studied. Those affected with the disease might experience severe mood swings or memory loss.

The science around head injuries was unknown during much of the league's history. During the early days, those hits to the head were known as "getting your bell rung." Often a player would take a hit to the head and keep playing. By 2013, people knew better. That year, the NFL reached an agreement with more than 18,000 former players. It agreed to pay up to $1 billion in total costs related to possible concussions those players sustained but were not treated for during their careers.

The science around concussions continues to evolve. Preventing them entirely might be impossible, but the league is trying to at least limit them. One way it's doing this is by educating players and officials. The goal is to ensure everyone is aware when a player has suffered a concussion, because players are more vulnerable to a second concussion if they go back on the field before the first one has healed.

A new concussion protocol should help. The protocol is a set of guidelines the league requires teams to follow during games. Two medical professionals

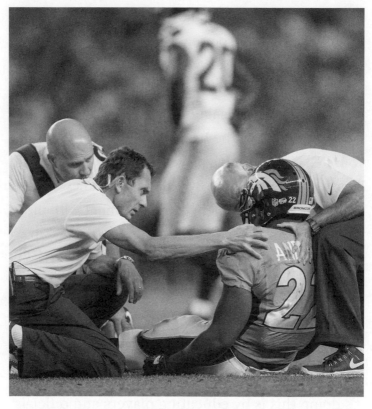

New protocols help ensure trainers know how to treat dangerous injuries such as concussions.

watch the game from high above the field. They have video equipment that lets them look at replays to determine if a player might have taken a shot to the head or could be dealing with concussion-like symptoms. Any player who might be dealing with a concussion is removed from the game and must undergo a series of tests. If the player is revealed to have a concussion, he cannot return to the playing field. These players also must complete a five-step process before they are cleared to practice.

The process starts with rest and recovery and slowly works its way up to full contact. There is no minimum or maximum time for the player to be in the protocol. Symptoms from some concussions disappear in a few days. Others linger for weeks, and some force players to retire early.

Advances in technology have helped NFL equipment become safer. The old leather helmets of the early days have been replaced by helmets that better absorb a blow to the head and in theory would lead to fewer concussions.

The coaches understand they, too, have a role to play in promoting safety. Pittsburgh Steelers coach Mike Tomlin tells his players, "Don't hit the head; don't use the head," a message he repeats to young players as part of the Heads Up program.

Tomlin stresses that it's important for the game to change with the times. There was a time when football coaches thought it was a good idea to limit water breaks during practice. No more.

New rules and equipment aim to keep the excitement in football for years to come.

"We laugh at [no water] now," Tomlin said. "It sounds medieval. The game is evolving, and I'm asking you to evolve with it." As the NFL embarked on its second century, the league had never been more

popular. The goal for the next 100 years is to make sure it stays that way. Having a safer league is an important part of the process.

To NFL fans, Sundays wouldn't be super without it.

SEATTLE
SEAHAWKS

OAKLAND/LAS VEGAS
RAIDERS

DENVER
BRONCOS

SAN FRANCISCO
49ERS

LOS ANGELES CHARGERS
LOS ANGELES RAMS

ARIZONA
CARDINALS

DALLAS
COWBOYS

HOUSTON TEX

NATIONAL FOOTBALL LEAGUE MAP

MINNESOTA
VIKINGS

GREEN BAY
PACKERS

DETROIT
LIONS

BUFFALO
BILLS

NEW ENGLAND
PATRIOTS

CHICAGO
BEARS

PITTSBURGH
STEELERS

NEW YORK GIANTS
NEW YORK JETS

CLEVELAND
BROWNS

INDIANAPOLIS
COLTS

PHILADELPHIA
EAGLES

KANSAS CITY
CHIEFS

CINCINNATI
BENGALS

WASHINGTON
REDSKINS

BALTIMORE
RAVENS

TENNESSEE
TITANS

CAROLINA
PANTHERS

ATLANTA
FALCONS

NEW ORLEANS
SAINTS

JACKSONVILLE
JAGUARS

TAMPA BAY
BUCCANEERS

MIAMI
DOLPHINS

TIMELINE

1892

William Heffelfinger becomes the first person to be paid to play football when the Allegheny Athletic Association pays him $500 to suit up for a game against the Pittsburgh Athletic Club on November 12.

1920

On September 17, the American Professional Football Association is formed.

1920

The Rock Island Independents beat the St. Paul Ideals 48–0 on September 26 in the first APFA game.

1922

The APFA changes its name to the National Football League.

1933

The NFL changes its rules to allow forward passes from anywhere behind the line of scrimmage, a move that revolutionizes the game.

1936

The Philadelphia Eagles select running back Jay Berwanger with the first pick in the first NFL Draft.

1946

Kenny Washington and Woody Strode sign with the Los Angeles Rams to become the first African American players in the NFL.

1951

The NFL championship game is carried on national television for the first time. The Los Angeles Rams beat the Cleveland Browns 24–17 on December 23.

1958

The first overtime playoff game ends with the Baltimore Colts beating the New York Giants 23–17 to win the NFL title on December 28.

1959

The American Football League is founded. The league debuts in 1960 with eight teams and adds two more teams in 1966.

1963

The first class of the Pro Football Hall of Fame is inducted in Canton, Ohio. The 17-member class includes icons such as George Halas, Sammy Baugh, and Red Grange.

1966

On June 8, the NFL and AFL agree to merge starting with the 1970 season.

1967

The Green Bay Packers beat the Kansas City Chiefs 35–10 on January 15 in the first Super Bowl.

1970

The Browns top the New York Jets 31–21 in the *Monday Night Football* debut on September 21.

1973

The Miami Dolphins defeat the Washington Redskins 14–7 in Super Bowl VII on January 14 to finish the season a perfect 17–0.

1982

More than 110 million people watch the San Francisco 49ers beat the Cincinnati Bengals in Super Bowl XVI on January 24, making it the most-watched sporting event in US television history at the time.

1993

The Dallas Cowboys win the Super Bowl on January 30, beginning a run of three championships in four seasons.

2002

Emmitt Smith passes Walter Payton to become the NFL's all-time leading rusher.

2008

The New York Giants upset New England 17–14 in the Super bowl on February 3 to end the Patriots' bid for a perfect season.

2009

The Pittsburgh Steelers hold off the Arizona Cardinals 27–23 in Super Bowl XLIII on February 1 to become the first team to win six Super Bowls.

2015

A record television audience of more than 114 million people watch the Patriots beat the Seattle Seahawks in Super Bowl XLIX on February 1.

2017

On February 5, New England rallies from 25 points down to beat Atlanta in overtime in Super Bowl LI. Tom Brady becomes the first quarterback to win five Super Bowls.

THE WINNERS

GREEN BAY PACKERS: 13 (four in Super Bowl era)

From Bart Starr to Brett Favre to Aaron Rodgers, the Packers have been fortunate to have some of the best quarterbacks in NFL history since the dawn of the Super Bowl era. Their 13 combined NFL and Super Bowl championships are also the most of any franchise.

CHICAGO BEARS: 9 (one in Super Bowl era)

No surprise that one of the league's original teams is also the franchise with the most wins in NFL history through the 2017 season, even if the Monsters of the Midway haven't played much like it during the Super Bowl era.

NEW YORK GIANTS: 8 (four in Super Bowl era)

The Giants, who won four league titles before the Super Bowl era, are consistent, having appeared in at least one Super Bowl every decade since the 1980s.

PITTSBURGH STEELERS: 6 (all in Super Bowl era)

Once one of the league's perennial losers, the Steelers are the winningest franchise of the Super Bowl era, having held the Vince Lombardi Trophy aloft six times entering the 2018 season.

NEW ENGLAND PATRIOTS: 5 (all in Super Bowl era)

Few expected much when Tom Brady took over as the Patriots' starting quarterback in 2001. Sixteen years later, Brady and coach Bill Belichick had won five Super Bowls together with the Patriots.

WASHINGTON REDSKINS: 5 (three in Super Bowl era)

The Redskins edge out longtime rivals the Philadelphia Eagles for fifth on the NFL's all-time wins list thanks mostly to their great run under Hall of Fame coach Joe Gibbs. Washington appeared in four Super Bowls under Gibbs, winning it all three times between the 1982 and 1991 seasons.

* Accurate through the 2017 NFL season.

THE BIG THREE

A collection of top performers in various statistics.

MOST HEAD COACHING WINS

1. Don Shula: 328
2. George Halas: 318
3. Tom Landry: 250
   Bill Belichick: 250

MOST CAREER PASSING YARDS

1. Peyton Manning: 71,940
2. Brett Favre: 71,838
3. Drew Brees: 70,445

MOST CAREER RUSHING YARDS

1. Emmitt Smith: 18,355
2. Walter Payton: 16,726
3. Barry Sanders: 15,269

MOST SINGLE-SEASON RUSHING YARDS

1. Eric Dickerson: 2,105
2. Adrian Peterson: 2,097
3. Jamal Lewis: 2,066

MOST CAREER RECEIVING YARDS

1. Jerry Rice: 22,895
2. Terrell Owens: 15,934
3. Larry Fitzgerald: 15,545

MOST CAREER TOUCHDOWNS

1. Jerry Rice: 208
2. Emmitt Smith: 175
3. LaDainian Tomlinson: 162

MOST CAREER SACKS
(*became official statistic in 1982)

1. Bruce Smith: 200
2. Reggie White: 198
3. Kevin Greene: 160

MOST CAREER POINTS

1. Morten Andersen: 2,544
2. Adam Vinatieri: 2,487
3. Gary Anderson: 2,434

* Accurate as of the 2017 NFL season.

FOR MORE INFORMATION

BOOKS

Anastasio, Dina. *What Is the Super Bowl?* New York: Grosset & Dunlap, 2015.

Graves, Will. *NFL's Top 10 Upsets.* Minneapolis: Abdo Publishing, 2018.

Scheff, Matt. *Amazing NFL Stories: 12 Highlights from NFL History.* Mankato, MN: 12-Story Library, 2016.

ON THE WEB

Associated Press NFL News
www.pro32.ap.org

NFL Rush: The League's Official Kids' Site
www.nflrush.com

Pro Football Hall of Fame
www.profootballhof.com

Pro Football Reference
www.profootballreference.com

PLACES TO VISIT

PRO FOOTBALL HALL OF FAME

2121 George Halas Dr. NW

Canton, OH 44708

330-456-8207

www.profootballhof.com

The Hall of Fame is like a museum dedicated to football. There are exhibits on the origin of the game, artifacts from famous moments, and busts honoring the greatest players and coaches ever.

LAMBEAU FIELD

1265 Lombardi Ave.

Green Bay, WI 54304

920-569-7500

www.packers.com/lambeau-field/index.html

The home of the Green Bay Packers is one of the oldest stadiums in the NFL, having been built in 1957. It is also the site of the Packers Hall of Fame, which features exhibits surrounding the history of the franchise and the many great players who have worn green and gold.

SELECT BIBLIOGRAPHY

BOOKS

Chicago Tribune Staff. *The Chicago Tribune Book of the Chicago Bears: A Decade-by-Decade History*. Chicago: Midway Books, 2015.

Editors of Sports Illustrated. *Sports Illustrated Football's Greatest Revised and Updated*. New York: Time Inc. Books, 2017.

Fischer, David. *The Super Bowl: The First Fifty Years of America's Greatest Game*. New York: Sports Publishing, 2015.

Kovacs, Vic. *Touchdown! The History of Football*. New York: Crabtree Publishing Co., 2018.

McAdam, Sean. *Boston: America's Best Sports Town*. Mendota Heights, MN: Press Box Books, 2018.

Rice, Jerry, and Randy O. Williams. *50 Years, 50 Moments: The Most Unforgettable Plays in Super Bowl History*. New York: Dey Street Books, 2015.

ONLINE

Holley, Joe, and Bart Barnes. "The First of the Gunslingers." *Washington Post*. 18 Dec. 2008. http://www.washingtonpost.com/wp-dyn/content/article/2008/12/17/AR2008121703347_2.html. Accessed 17 Nov. 2017.

Katzowitz, Josh. "Remember When: 'Greatest Game Ever Played' Still Impacts NFL." *cbssports.com*. 27 Dec. 2013. https://www.cbssports.com/nfl/news/remember-when-greatest-game-ever-played-still-impacts-nfl/. Accessed 17 Nov. 2017.

Labriola, Bob. "Tomlin Issues Call-To-Arms to HS Coaches." *steelers.com*. 7 Apr. 2016. http://www.steelers.com/news/article-1/Tomlin-issuescall-to-arms-to-HS-coaches/41cd01a6-4a78-4e94-9056-92b191e4a14f. Accessed 17 Nov. 2017.

Litzky, Frank. "Don Hutson, Star Pass-Catcher, Dies at 84." *New York Times*. 26 June 1997. http://www.nytimes.com/1997/06/27/sports/don-hutson-star-pass-catcher-dies-at-84.html. Accessed 17 Nov. 2017.

INDEX

ABOUT THE AUTHOR

Will Graves became hooked on the NFL after attending the 1982 NFC Championship Game between the Washington Redskins and the Dallas Cowboys. Graves watched his beloved Redskins win the Super Bowl three times before he graduated high school. More than 25 years later, he's still waiting for Washington to get back on top. Graves has spent more than two decades as a sports writer, covering the NFL, professional baseball, hockey, and the Olympics for the Associated Press in Pittsburgh, Pennsylvania, where he lives with his wife and two children.